West Virginia

ABC Coloring Book

An ABC Learning Activity Book all about West Virginia

With Count-to-10 Coloring Bonus!

Little Red Hills

Written & designed by: Rianna M. Hill

www.WyomingisHome.com

Wyoming Is Home is a Brand of

Little Red Hills LLC

My ABCs West Virginia Coloring Book

name:

A

American

Black Bear

The black bear is the state animal of West Virginia and can be found throughout the state's forests and mountains.

B

Bald Eagle

This majestic bird of prey is a symbol of the United States and can be spotted in West Virginia, especially near water bodies.

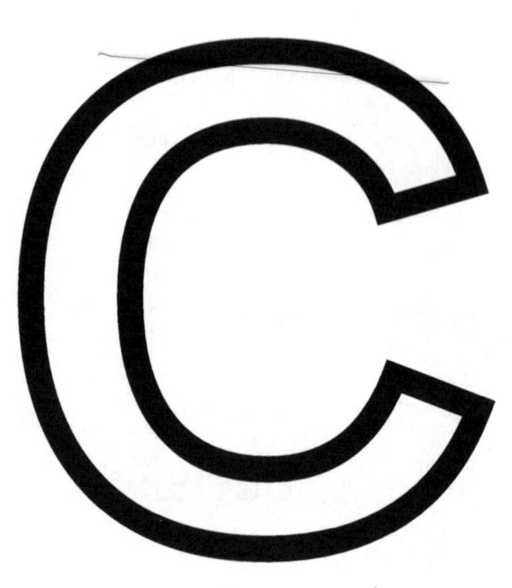

Cooper's Hawk

A medium-sized bird of prey known for its agility in flight, the Cooper's hawk can be found in West Virginia's woodlands.

D

Deer

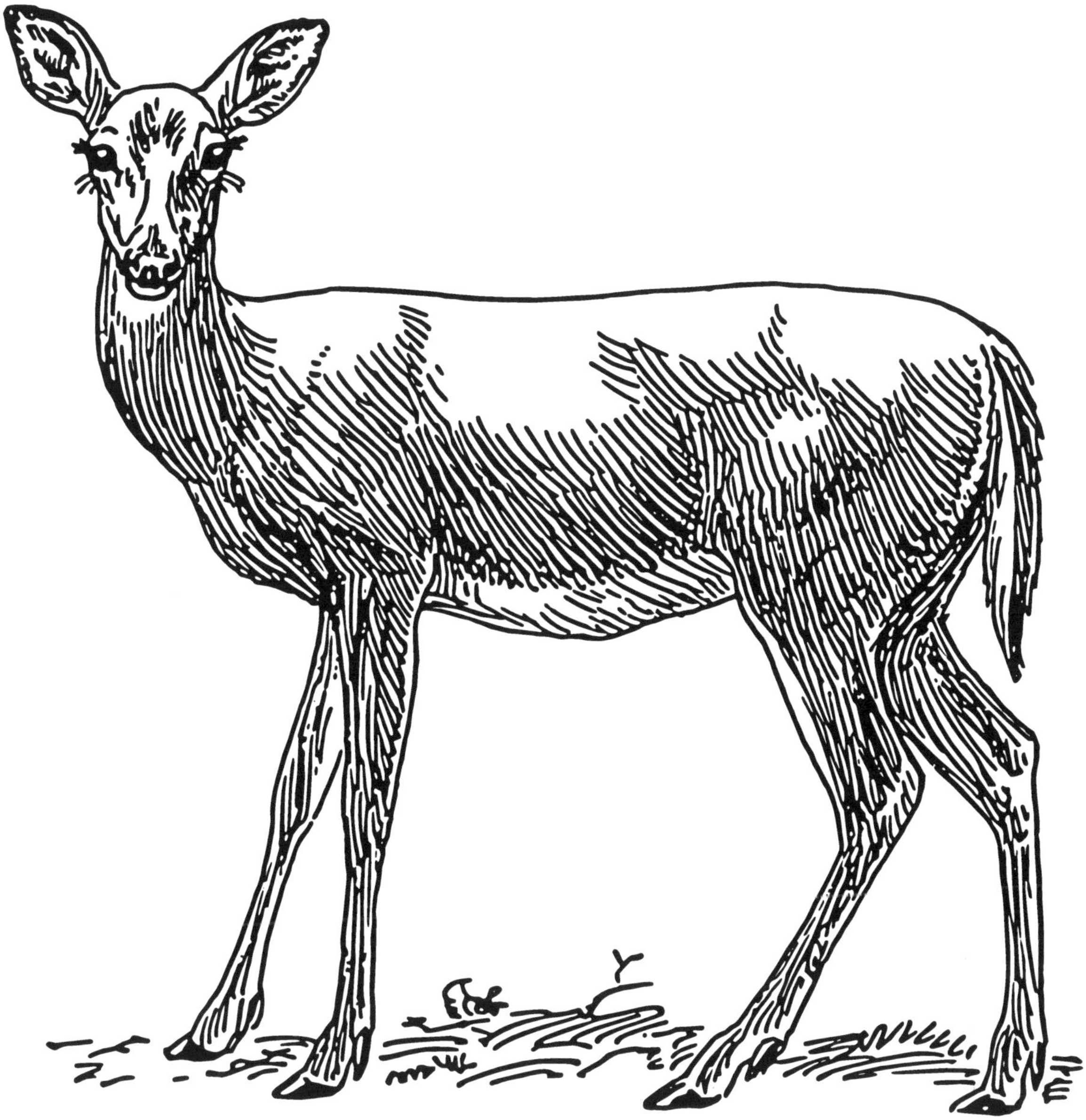

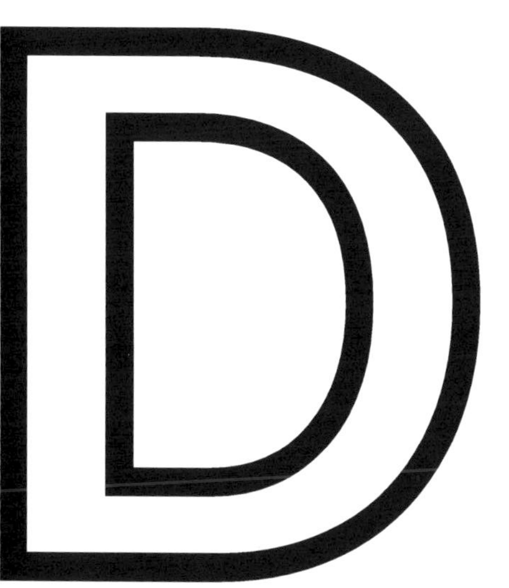

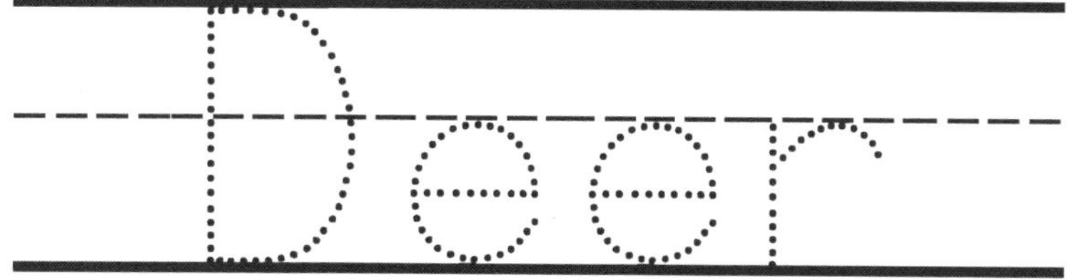

White-tailed deer are common in West Virginia and are popular game animals.

E

Eastern Box Turtle

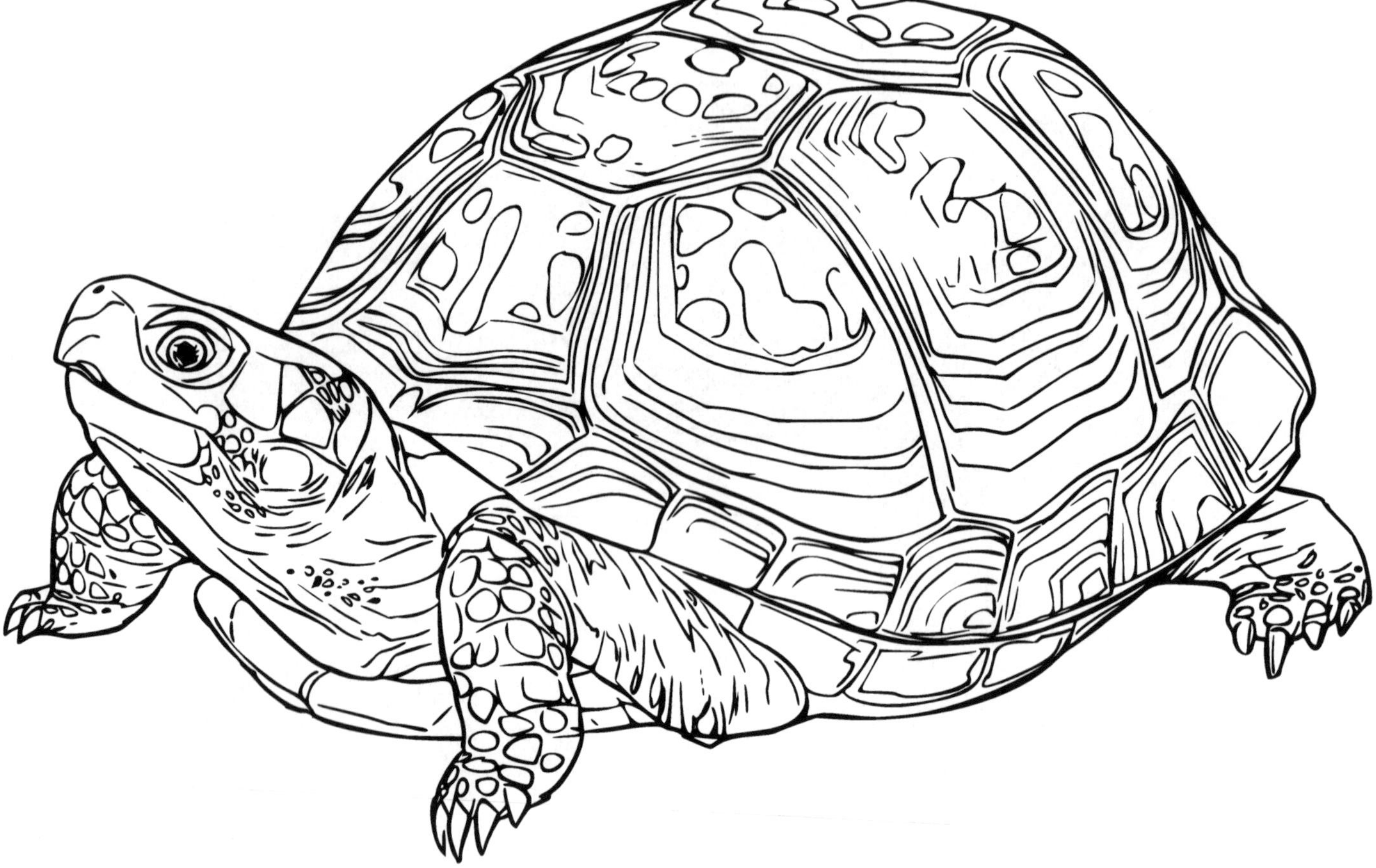

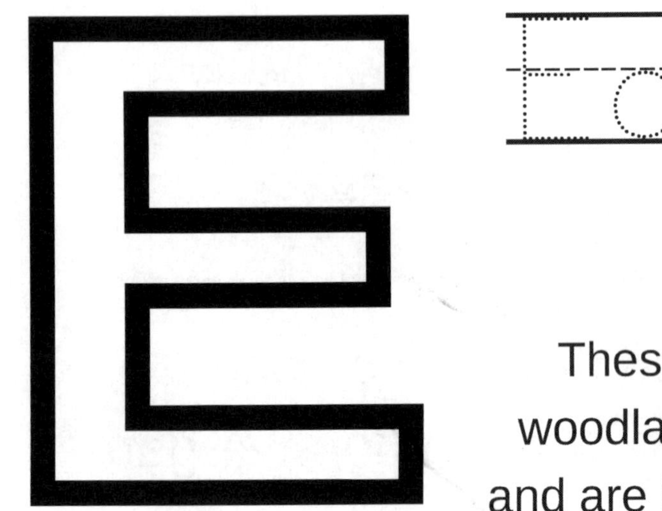

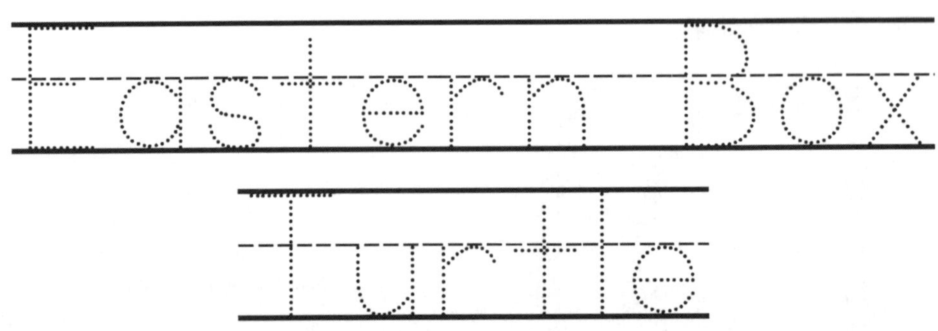

These terrestrial turtles are found in the woodlands and grasslands of West Virginia and are known for their distinctive box-shaped shells.

F

Fisher

Also known as fisher cats, these carnivorous mammals are known for their sleek appearance and are found in West Virginia's forests.

G

Gray Fox

These small canids are known for their gray fur and can be found in the woodlands and rural areas of the state.

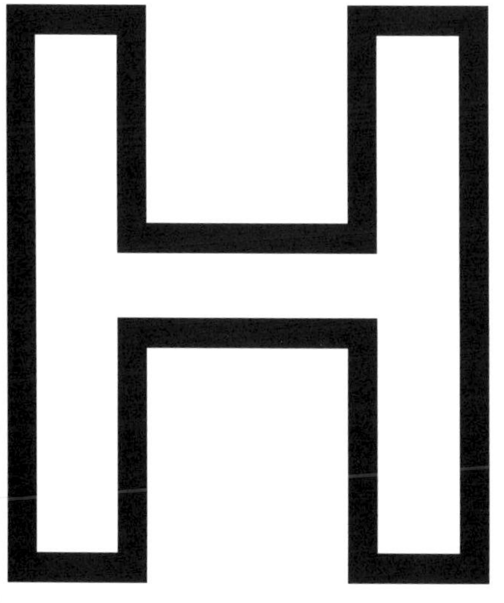

Hellbender

Salamander

The Eastern hellbender is a large, aquatic salamander found in West Virginia's clean, fast-flowing streams.

I

Indigo Bunting

A brightly colored bird with brilliant blue plumage, the indigo bunting is often seen in West Virginia's open woodlands and grasslands.

This small, lungless salamander is found in the forests and woodlands of West Virginia.

The American kestrel is a small falcon known for its striking plumage and can be found in open country areas.

L

Long-tailed
Weasel

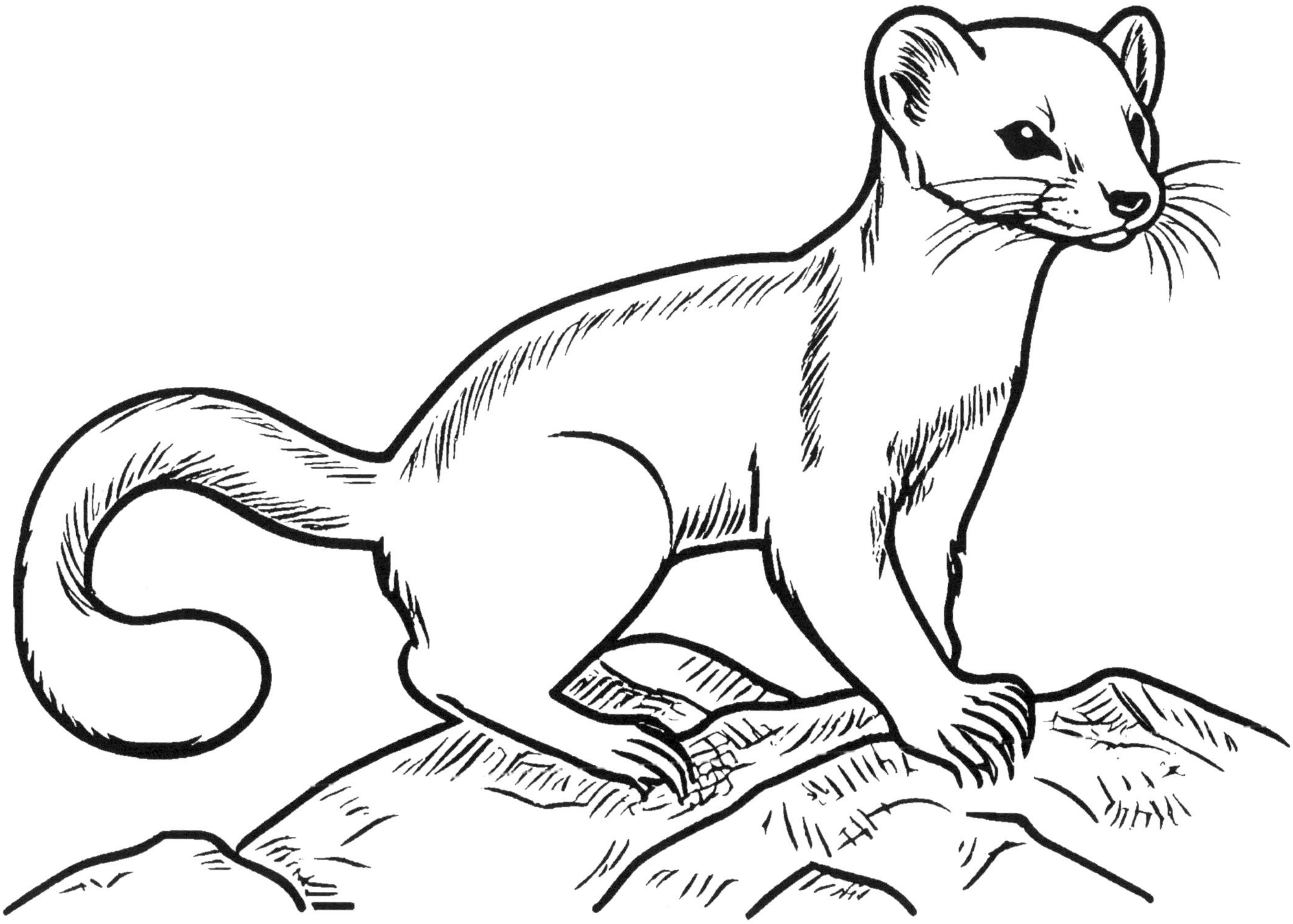

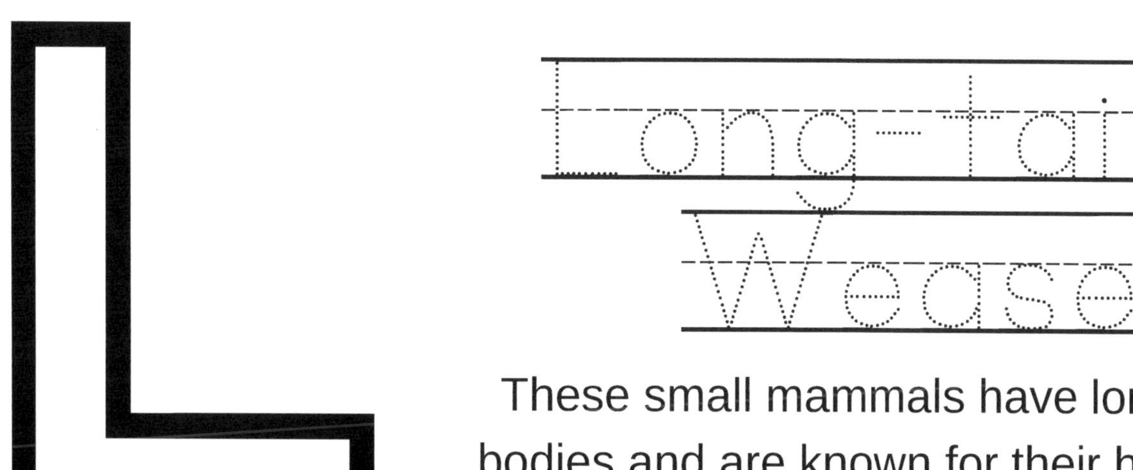

These small mammals have long, slender bodies and are known for their hunting skills in West Virginia's woodlands.

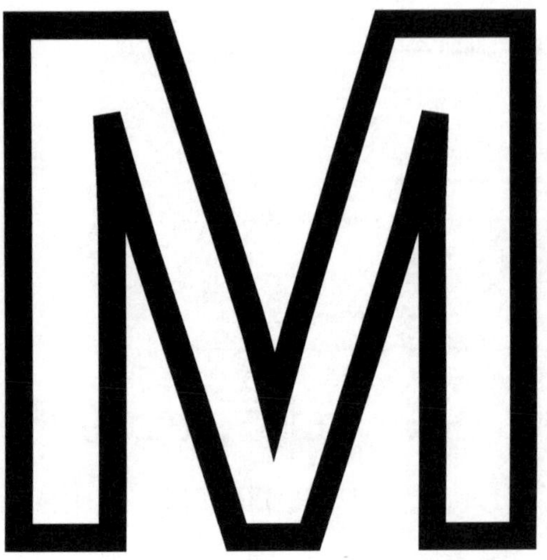

Mountain Lion

Also known as cougars or pumas, mountain lions are elusive big cats that may occasionally pass through the state.

Northern Water Snake

These non-venomous snakes can be found in West Virginia's water bodies, and they are known for their semi-aquatic lifestyle.

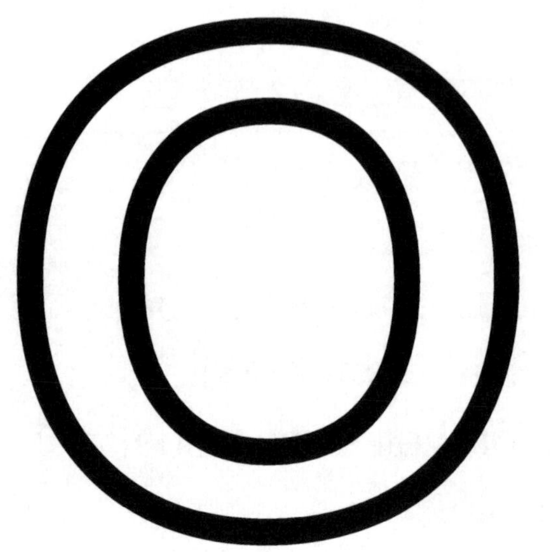

Osprey

A bird of prey known for its fishing abilities, ospreys can be seen near water bodies in West Virginia.

The peregrine falcon is a swift and powerful raptor that can be seen in West Virginia's mountainous areas.

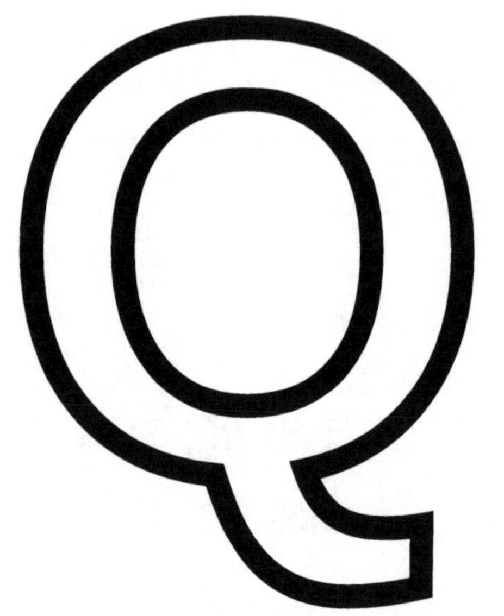

Quail

Northern bobwhite quail are ground-dwelling birds found in grasslands and agricultural areas of West Virginia.

Red Fox

These beautiful mammals are known for their reddish-orange fur and are found in rural and wooded areas.

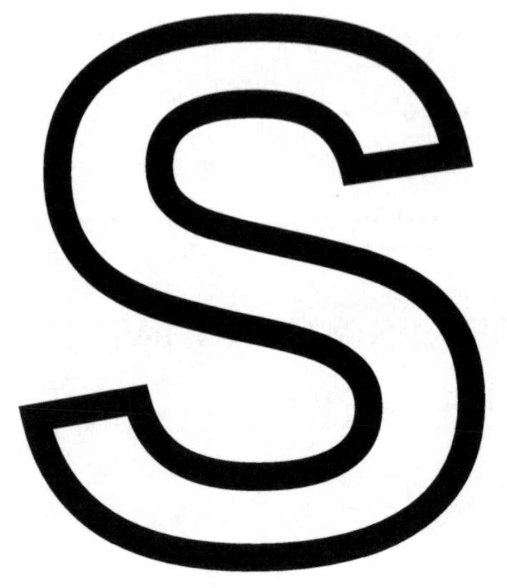

Spotted
Salamander

These black with yellow spots amphibians can be found in woodlands and wetlands of West Virginia.

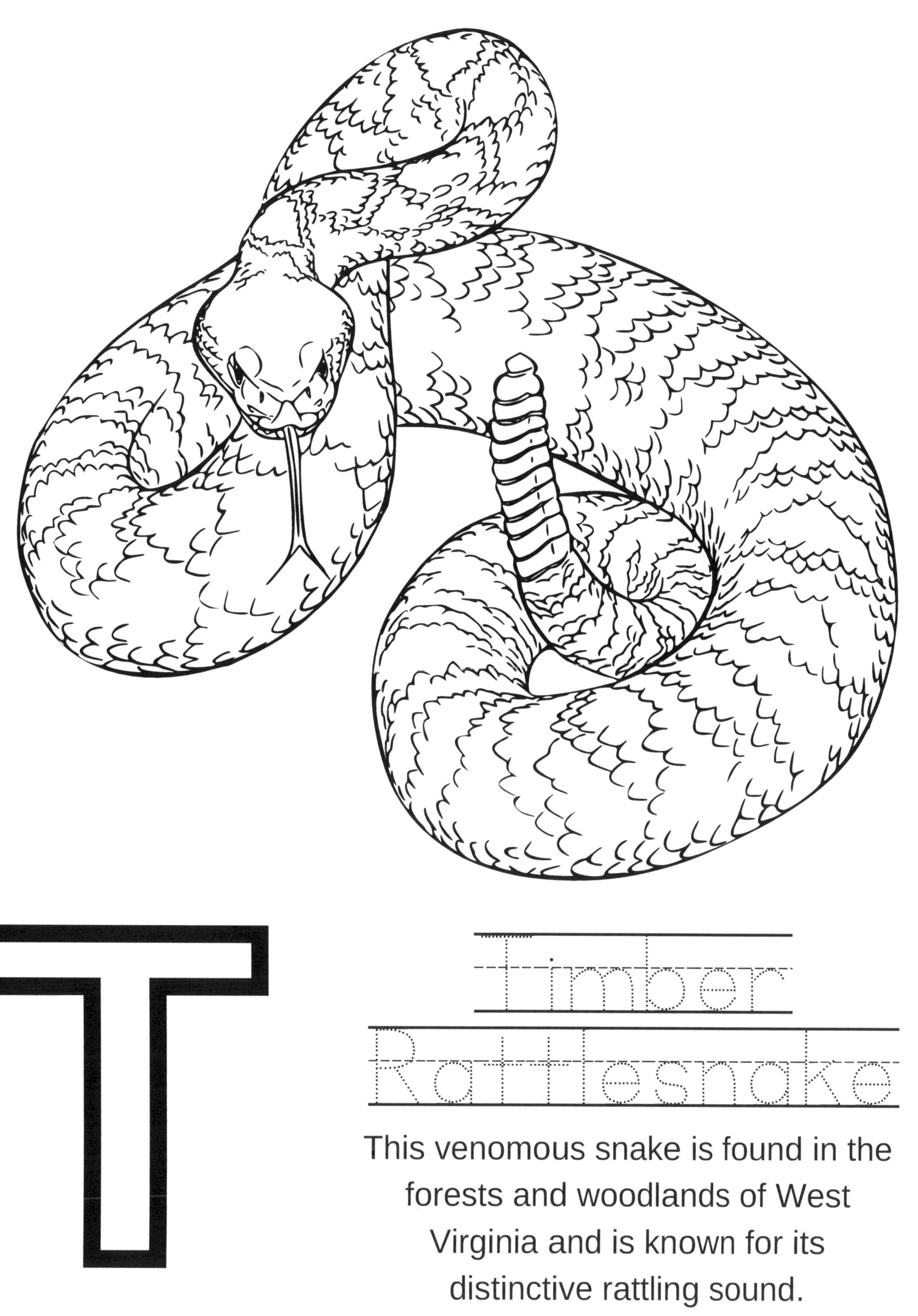

This venomous snake is found in the forests and woodlands of West Virginia and is known for its distinctive rattling sound.

U

Upland Sandpiper

A medium-sized shorebird, the upland sandpiper can be found in grasslands and open fields in West Virginia.

V

Vulture

Turkey vultures and black vultures are scavenger birds often seen soaring in the skies of West Virginia.

Wood Duck

Known for their colorful plumage, wood ducks are often seen in wetlands and wooded areas of the state.

X

Xenopus Frog

Although not native to West Virginia, this species of frog has been introduced into some water bodies in the state.

Yellow Warbler

A small, yellow bird, the yellow warbler can be seen in riparian habitats and wetlands in West Virginia.

Z

Zebra Swallowtail Butterfly

This distinctive butterfly with black and white stripes can be found in West Virginia's woodlands and meadows.

MY COUNT TO 10 WEST VIRGINIA ANIMALS COLORING BOOK

name: ______________________________

1

one eagle

2

two deers

3

three hawks

4

four turtles

5

five salamanders

6

six foxes

7

seven lions

8

eight quails

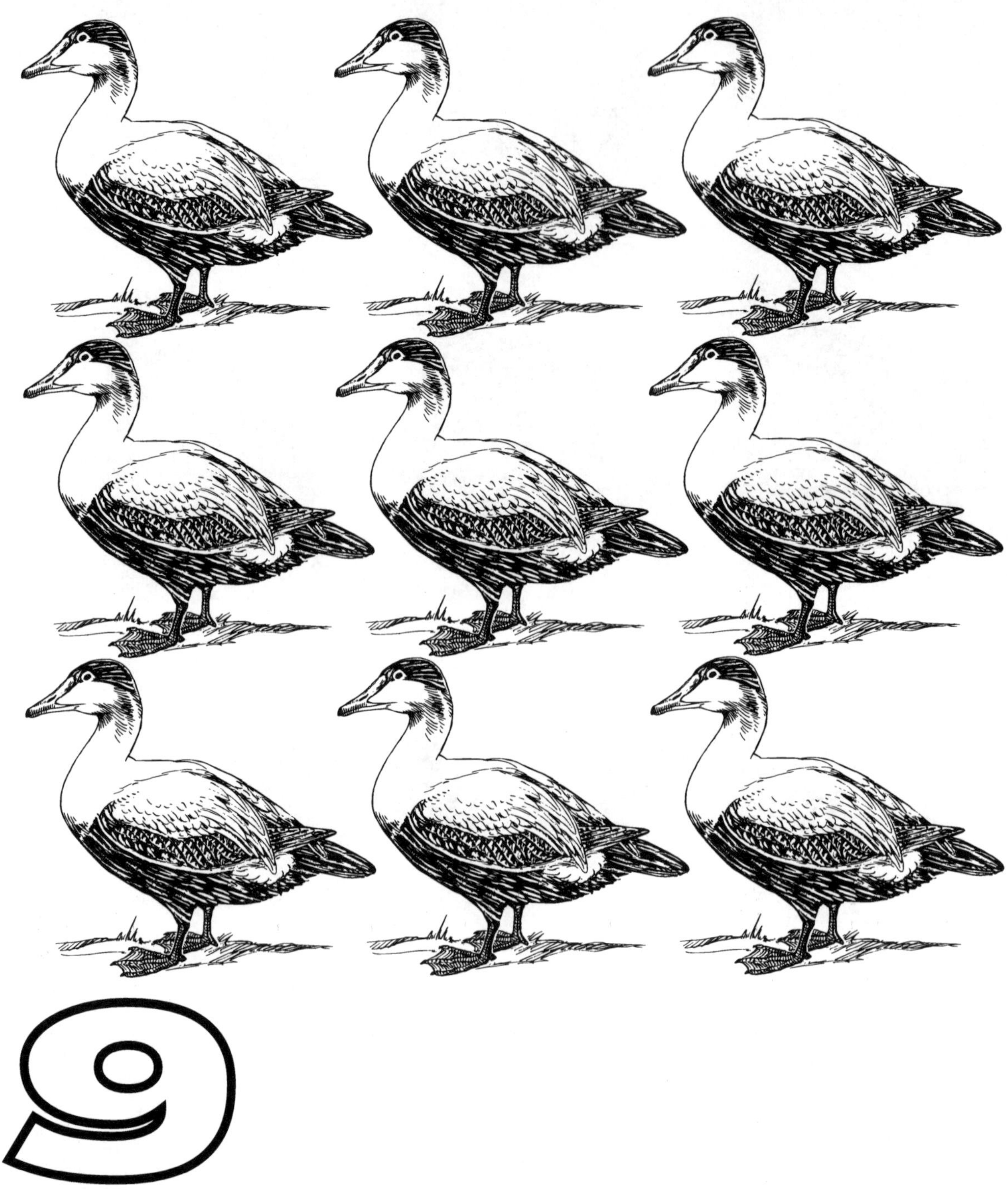

9

nine ducks

10
ten butterflies

Thank you for supporting our small family business!

Learn more at:

www.WyomingisHome.com

Questions or
suggestions for improvement?

Rianna@LittleRedHills.com

Wholesale order questions for
your shop?

Rianna@LittleRedHills.com

Made in the USA
Middletown, DE
17 August 2024